The Repeater

For Charlie
For Rhonda
For Rachel

The Smell of Rain on Dust

Growing up in a place that doesn't exist does strange
things to a body. Certain corners of New Jersey are a
sprawling web of cornfields-turned-subdivisions, with the
fabled, eccentric artery of Rt. 9 cutting through it; a
conveyor belt that took our daddies to The City before
the sun came up, and brought them home long after our
bedtimes ticked by. Our tired eyes lit out across well-
manicured lawns, waiting for equally tired headlights to
swing the corner into the drive.

My birth certificate boasts the seal of New York, but it
was the soft whirr of crickets praying to their secret gods
that lulled me to sleep in the summers. It was never the
echo of cars and people in their endless motion, hustling

like the insects in the soft grass. Oblivious in their valleys and canyons. Both moving to the ancient patterns shaped by geography and instinct.

We hunted the empty places for fireflies and swam in our own blue pools. The neighbors would come, and the men would drink beer together and laugh at themselves. The women sipped wine or iced tea while we ran amok; our soles gone leather from a barefoot month, gulping mouthfuls from the garden hose - and sometimes turning our faces to fountains; aiming for each other with the messy, buckshot accuracy of children.

We were gluttons for the summer, and we drank in the deep, humid days with the same greedy abandon that our parents swallowed their long summer cocktails and canned domestics.

We picked our mosquito bites and our noses, and the earth spun hard enough on it's eternal axis to make the sky fiery through the leaves. When the ultramarine of the open ocean loomed above us as we craned our necks and bodies. We would go indoors and wash the deet and chlorine off of ourselves, like roman soldiers returning from a long campaign. Our skin returned to us as grey water circled the drains.

Our pictures were snapped with disposable birthday cameras and we lost our teeth in candy hoarded from brightly printed cellophane goody bags; lovingly wrapped by the mother of this friend or that friend. Our lives were plastics in primary colors and cotton blends in splashes of neon.

Neighborhood dogs herded us, and we loved them like we were told God loved all - equally and without judgement; even when they covered us in mud and fur and spit in their excitement; in their eagerness to prove that the world would go on forever, and that we were perfect for always to them.

The construct of our daily motion was a constant shift from vehicle to building to soccer field to underwear to uniform to bathing suit to pajamas. A frenzy of hands and hair ties. The cacophony of beat-up sneakers running from one end of the polished hardwood floor in a state-funded gym to the other.

Peals of laughter. Someone told a dirty joke or whispered a word that only the adult world was privy to. The raised eyebrows of the code-breaker as they waited for the reaction of the crowd. A Discovery. Secret. Hands hiding smiles that eyes gave away.

Shrieks of agony. Tears. The sudden stillness of children absorbing their own mortality. A plaster cast covered in hearts and names. Standing guard. Letters scrawled in bright sharpie marker. Our graffiti; a waving, sacred testament.

But none of it existed.

Big Lonesome & The Sideways Sun

The inherent isolation of a childhood partitioned by high fences and busy highways turns people strange. We were kings; lords of driftwood empires. Champions of hardscrabble lots. We were bastard demigods climbing piles of abandoned construction debris that served as our Olympus. We were monsters and tigers. Creeks and overflow ponds echoed with our battle cries. We were mermen and pirates. We were cowboys and indians and wild horses.

The tips of our guns were hot, and our hammers always clicking.

We were cannon fodder for each other's wildest dreams.

As adults, the voices of our neighbors still sift excitedly through shafts of light cast by a tired sun on a rolling September breeze.

Autumn was a thief that stole our dark skin and our savagery. It was new shoes to soften the pads of our asphalt-toughened feet. It was hours dedicated to the mall for new clothing, because last year's simply felt worn.

New everything. Our mothers were replacing their children with second chances. Crumpled lists from our teachers in one hand, and the stroller handle, bags full of the smell of fresh garment dye, or the hand of their child in the other.

Our mothers spending the hard-won dollars that filtered down the turnpike from Metropolis. From Gotham.

The same conversation, everywhere. Flamingoes at the waterhole.

"Just try it on for size. You don't have to like the color."

"She has a very wide foot and a very high instep."

"We're going to stop feeding him this year if he keeps growing out of his clothes this fast."

"What are you talking about, I see kids wearing this style all the time."

And my mother, the commander.

In her deafness, she became single-minded and overbearing when confronted by the back-to-school migration.

"I know you're tired, I'm tired, too - oh! Hi Joanne. Same here. Yes, we're doing back-to-school a bit late, I know...the sales are still good here, not that..."

"Not as good as South? What? What? Oh, every year a little bit later. Gotta run. Dinner is going to be so late. Bye Joanne."

"Did you hear what she said at the end there? I couldn't catch it. She mumbles. Pizza tonight."

My mother, always catching everything, or trying to. A constant block-and-tackle of syllables as they flew at her. She read lips as easily as she breathed, with only the occasional cough or hiccup.

After every social interaction, especially public, unexpected ones, her face would slip down into distraction. She would look as though she were studying maps of an unknown continent, printed in another language. She was carefully reviewing, logging information, and making sure she didn't misread the mouths of the other party. She could see people's conversations the way we see our fingertips on the opposite wall of a fish tank. A surface that appears transparent and clear until pressed.

The awkward small talk of our parents becomes our own. Folded into us like a salt vein in the stone. Nervous tics and temper tantrums. We are the living legacies of bad habits and poor manners. The ability to remember and recall full conversations and stories rests here.

The fall was groggy mornings, progressively colder and darker. Wet leaves clinging to the sidewalk in an ecstatic carpet of warm colors.

Lazy afternoons spent peeling horse glue off of our hands, and the smell of erasers. The rapid-fire tapping on the chalkboard, and the yellow hulks of school buses with their parallel lines of children in parallel rows of seats.

The Skyline, the Treeline

In the subdivision, every property was gifted a willow tree and a Japanese maple. Willow trees stationed in the back yard; tall and looming, with great, powerful branches swaying ever upward from a weird, stunted trunk.

It was only in my late adolescence that I learned that willow trees grow underwater, and the men who designed my development knew they had doomed these haunted, beautiful things to early graves in the sandy clay of the filled-in marsh upon which our houses stood.

They knew, and they built and planted, anyway. Vanity is never kind, never true, always shortsighted, and has farther-reaching consequences than any of it's practitioners can ever foresee.

My father falling. Racing towards the ground against what was the highest willow branch in creation; dropping from the sky like a felled swan. That is the oldest image I hold. Watching with watery panic and screaming for a mother who refused to believe me. Refused to turn her head to see outside and witness with me.

My father, king of my world, had climbed to trim the branches of the willow that grew up and out of our muddled earth. It's lanky, lazy limbs would sway ponderously in the summer storms, and it worried him, for the safety of the fence that surrounded our property.

Up he went and down he came.

I remember my dad's wails of agony and anger as my mother ran out into the hot sun. I remember being blinded momentarily by the chrome-white sunburst on the porch door. I remember our neighbor scooping me into her arms and carrying me away. I remember all of these fragments, but I remember the day his cast came off most clearly. Trauma has a way of leaving the deepest impressions when the curtains come up and when they fall. The show in between these points is usually blurry, muffled, and best left that way.

The hip-to-toe plaster cast which he had to wear for a month was covered in crayon and marker. We would sit in the garage. He on a stool, the crutches set against his table while he tinkered; and me on the floor, drawing flowers and birds and sunshine and fishes on his leg. I decorated my dad, because I loved him so. The more happiness I placed on the cast, the faster his leg would heal. This is the logic of children. Love heals all. I was an urchin in ancient Rome, littering the pantheon with marks. I was a sailor on the grey atlantic, carving my heart into the tooth of a whale. The pylon of his long leg served as my canvas, and I drew for him every beautiful thing I knew.

When the time came for the doctor to cut the cast off of him, we went, the three of us, my mother holding me gently. I remember my dad lying calmly on the table, and then I was jarred into hysterics by the doctor wielding a machine that produced a constant metallic scream. The plaster saw.

I knew they were going to kill him.

I could see it in my minds eye that screaming machine plunging into my dad. It would eat him. The noise alone could kill. And then they closed the door.

Adults never explain what's going to happen next to children - especially if they think it's going to be unpleasant. The human pattern of cleaning up the mess as opposed to preventing the mess in the first place. We are locked in a kiss with chaos on our deepest levels. The mistake of telling a child that it is OK, instead of it's going to be OK is the dark little worm at the center of so much unnecessary pain. The tiny knots around which the muscles of our memories grow misshapen and useless.

The cast came off. My father came out of the terrible little room. His leg was matted and pale, and he held me for a very long time.

He limped for the rest of his life.

The Japanese maples did not fare much better. Ours was the last one to die on our street. This was due to my father's incredible aptitude for engaging the invasive species of beetle that called The Maple both home and harvest, in a tenacious and personal form of trench warfare. He would choose a poison. The beetle would adapt. He would buy traps. The beetle would find a way out. He would fire the leaves. The beetle would eat the ones left.

Eventually, like his grandfather before him, my father had driven his force out and over the top so many times, that there was nothing left to fight for.

An accidental scorched earth campaign.

The maple's remaining leaves withered, the trunk collapsed in on itself from months of chemical dosing, and with tears in his eyes, the man brought down it's desecrated corpse.

Christ was brought down from his cross as gently as my dad felled this tree.

When he cut through most of it's brittle, dead trunk, he stopped the chainsaw's engine, placed the ugly, biting machine at his feet, and took the tree down with his hands. All it took was a single push. There was a snap like the sound of an open hand across an unguarded face, and my father on one knee, cradling his failure. Beetles; their backs pearlescent, shimmering tears of sapphire and onyx poured out of the tree, and his hands were steady.

It took less than a minute to break the trunk into sections, and the scant canopy was quick work for the chainsaw, but the remains of The Maple sat on the front lawn for two long August days before it was approached again, fully dismantled, and bundled at the curb.

It was a wake. It was a mourning time for the loss of something beautiful and dear.
It is only in our own sea of loss that we come to recognize the pains our parents suffered.

We will always transpose ourselves. Lay our bodies and lives over the ones that came before us. We will always reach to adapt, no matter how alien the environment. No matter how impossible it may be the push to chameleon, we try. The soil is too shallow. The trunk is too porous. The water is too high.

The sky is too open.

In Granite

The New York City skyline is God's picket fence. The Verrazano bridge is a string of pearls laced across the throat of the night. Glass and steel and endless concrete float up from the horizon like islands in the sky as we near the city. The Turnpike is oily and darkened by the light rain. The smell of asphalt changing temperature. The smell of the other cars. The bass rattling Japanese frames as they beat by the toll booths.

A root system takes hold in the pit of my stomach. The buildings rise up, shaking their faces in defiance at the clouds. They do not see us, in their infinity. What would we do of the New York City skyline suddenly shifted and focused its incredible, collective attention on us? What waits on the other side of the tunnel? Will New York swallow us whole, all gnashing teeth and ferocity? Would it wrap us in eight million pairs of arms and lull us to sleep in soft rain and thrumming sidewalks? It will kiss us good night with an updraft from the antechambers below. Show us color. Show us rhythm. Hold up a mirror. The city was a dangerous gift to be unwrapped, new each time. We were reverse-pioneering, walking along the spine of a giant.

The long, graceful swoop of highway that leads to the Lincoln Tunnel is framed by an outcropping of the same glacial rock that supports the island of Manhattan. The turtle's shell. The shoulders of Atlas. They are graffitied a thousand times over. Proclamations of love. Promises of hatred, declarations of identity all running together in an idiot chorus. Screaming to the sky. To the traffic. To the strangers, saying "I was here. This was me."

A fading Grateful Dead skull meant as a farewell to Jerry Garcia. It appeared there when I was small. It is one of my earliest memories of New York before it was new. Someone's sacred memorial.

There are trees growing in the cracks of the rocks, now. Stunted and scrawny, but fighting for the light and flourishing in the black granite. Left unchecked, their roots will crack their captors. We are stone-marooned trees, all of us, and we are old as tears.

Caterpillar

There were the still places, long untouched by machines, and we found them all. The felled trees and cinderblocks we used as forts and castles in the gemstone summers of childhood became bench seating. Became ashtrays. Became sacrificial altars. Gateways out of innocence.

A pile of bikes and the odd car at the edge of a clearing, where a nearly invisible hole in the tree line lead to the would-be foundation of a house.

We smoked cigarettes until our lungs were sore. Our stomachs gone sour from cheap beer hustled out of this guy's brother last night. Our tongues dry and our eyes red from the dirt weed we scored from the kids in The

Harbor. All parts of us stood ready. We thrashed and danced in a fog of teenage anticipation.

The frenzy of laughter - genuine, nervous, and stoned - bouncing off of the half-built walls. Clothing hanging on branches. Our new bodies slipping into the cold water of the quarry. Picking gingerly through the reeds, sliding on our toes. The hoots of the boys as they surfaced; the wild cries of the girls as they were splashed and goaded into the black water. Cicadas and tree frogs singing with us. Shaking our hair for bugs and keeping the lips of our bottles above the surface of the water. Everything around us glowed in the green-filtered sun. The summer was a cathedral, and we were devout in our worship.

There were three ledges, a spiral staircase to an open sky. Two natural platforms which jutted out like shattered teeth from the stone walls of the quarry. The highest one was barely visible from the ground and obscured by treetops. It hung over the water and stone like the head of a bird of prey. The middle sister was broken and stunted. To clear the treachery below, and make it to the water, we had to run and leap and hope. The little sister, the lowest ledge, only rose about ten feet off the ground - the height of our parent's garages. It was one ancient wood plank; a tree trunk sawed in half, stapled with mold-blackened berber carpeting and half-buried in the earth that ran up to the open maw of the crater wall.

Each one higher and more dangerous. Each one a dare.

We threw ourselves from them and tumbled into oblivion. Legs bending to the sky, chests and stomachs tight, full of moving parts, launched out, out, and downward to kiss terminal velocity before the water folded us into it's mystery. Screaming for nothing and everything. Our hearts were always falling.

Feeling for the underwater stone ledge with our feet. Running our toes along the drop, slick with algae, unable to see past our thighs in the murk. The sensation of standing on the edge of a wilderness into which you could fall forever. Sink until the surface was a pinhole of light through your fingertips.

I was always the last in and the last out. Watching the water churn around my friends. Watching them turn to Selkies in the bottomless crater. What I buried my heart in deepest was having the quarry to myself. It was ritual. The boys would climb out, all simian bravado; flinging water at each other and playing keep-away with towels. The girls would follow, their faces suddenly too aware of their relative nudity. As though leaving the water left them more vulnerable. The shock of the air turning us coltish and graceless.

The water would calm as I laid on my back, floating. There was no current, no pulse in the water, save for mine. I would keep my ears in, to hear my steady breath and verify my heart was still there. I would stare up at the shifting kaleidoscopic ceiling. The immense transept formed by the maples around the edge of the quarry created pillars of light that plunged all the way down into the water. If you were waiting for it, you could see the shadow of something with gills and unblinking eyes drift through them. Bugs and dust in galaxies around me. Everything in perfect time with everything else. It was all a symphony.

The rusted hulk of the CAT that was abandoned at this half-finished home lent itself to impromptu dressing rooms and drying racks. It's yellow body falling to the forces of entropy. Birds nests lovingly wedged into the treads over the months. Vines crawled delicately up the dust-heavy cabin windows, and the toothed scoop of the earth mover had filled with rain so often that Spring, that the weight had snapped it at the hinge.

Everything falls. All things eventually slump over and sink back into the earth, gently forgotten.

Squids and Whales

Our limbs stretched out to the points of the compass.
Our round jaws grew edged as we chewed gum and
smoked our first cigarettes. We caged our teeth and
banded them in rainbows. Retainers and contact lenses.
Deodorant and cologne and perfume. Hair spray and
make-up clutches. We became totems of plastic and
chemicals. A cascade of faces leaning into spotted
bathroom mirrors. Dipping forward and back. Davening
at the wall of vanity. The constant volley of insults and
compliments and questions and whispers.
Hummingbirds in the garden. The highway of discourse
in the kingdom of the newly-teenaged female is a dimly
lit four-leaf-clover that folds in on itself twice.

The tongues of girls pushing air and spit through braces
and Chapstick. Filling membranes of spearmint with
muscle and snapping it to punctuate the murmur in the
stalls and corridors and stairwells. The older we got, the
more walls we found around us. Adolescence was a

claustrophobic, blurry operetta set to the orchestra of emptied, open places where we were no longer allowed to play.

We were satellites in the vacuum. Set adrift by forces we didn't understand, hurtling towards a destination we knew nothing of, and helpless to stop it. Patashniks, all, drifting into the black. Waist-high in our sea-changes, we began to pair up. Create our own gravity and heat around cores lit phosphorous white and soft in all of that dark, static cold.

The fluid crusade, all hands and mouths and waistlines and collarbones. In dimly lit basements, surrounded by forests of wood paneling and our parent's ever-increasingly watered-down liquor. This is how we found us. In laundry rooms. In frantic, unlocked bathrooms with our backs as barricades. This is how we found us. With the fatalistic determination of kamikaze pilots, we barreled our kisses and our hands into each others' mouths and pockets. In the back seats of first cars. Our legs covered in sand, and our hair full of sun. This is how we found us.

This is how we found our bodies in each others' bodies.

I slid my fingers into her, and kept them there until they ached. I was full of sweet, sap-rolled liquor because it tasted good, and I didn't know any better. I was full of her for the same reasons. Her white belly and long neck. Her legs parting for me. Her teeth in my shoulder. Her mouth sealed to mine and her breath, all ethyl and hormones and heat, flooding my nose. My lungs. My blood. Everything becoming an endless pulse of want.

We weren't even women, yet.

I would fight everything. For you, I would crawl over coals. I know nothing but this. I would kneel before any god if it meant I could worship at your altar. I know nothing. I am lost.
This is first love. This is a heart cracked open, not to bleed; but to bloom like a bulb in a pit of soft, ready earth.

Her black hair between my flexing fingers. Her mouth, her wiry hands and hot skin against every part of me that mattered. In bedrooms still lined with magazine pages and pastels. Floral sheets still suffering the death knells of childhood. Beds still made for one body. Stifling our throats. Catching every note of swan song between our teeth. Grabbing each breath and holding it. Forcing it into the other's mouth and letting our voices crack the heavy pauses.

My heels digging into the back of her heart.

When the universe was young, or in the anti-moments before it became, and everything tore apart in the violence, I think our atoms were close to each other. I think we have been seeking us out since then. Trying, across space and through time, at a molecular level, to knit existence back together.

We had only the one night before the world crowbarred itself between us. Before the walls went up, and the phone calls came. In the moments before it all ripped itself to pieces again, we were so close.

The threats rolling down on all sides from the adults crashed over us. Our homes became avalanche zones, and we grew quiet, so as not to trigger them. Speaking to each other was a feat of incredible bravery and defiance. It required the timing and cunning usually employed by upper-echelon military operatives. The Cold War we left in our wake would build the bulwark that drives my heart to sink into everything with the weight of water.

We became clandestine agents, engaged in espionage both for and against the warring houses of our parents. Her mother pulled her from school. Soon after that, I was kicked out. Tantrums and rage. The complete violation by this first and total loss. I was on fire for months. Was a pacing, screaming animal. Was a home-made mortar before I centered myself, and wits won over temper.

The fallout, the lawsuits, the secrets, and the tumult of our spiraling hearts blowing outward and spinning into constellations.

A hushed phone call to guide me to you. A time and a place. A stolen car through the sprawl. For you. I love you, as they pull us from each other, yelling over our heads and grabbing our shoulders. Arms. Wrists. Engines idling. I love you as they throw you in the car, as they scream in your face, which looks only at me, and smiles. I love you as the hands rain down across my jaw, and the tears follow.

I love you years later, when we are both women. When you find me again, and show me everyone I never knew I was missing. Now you are many years gone. Your fine and lovely body placed in a fire, and then a porcelain jar, as smooth as teeth. But I don't think of it that way. I know that you're In Rainbows. Like a lost pilot, you flew your mission into the rainbows, and you are having adventures on the other side of them, wherever they go.

I see you through the veil of things that never happened.

Echo Down the Line

When a parent dies, there is an essential nakedness
that comes. The dropping of a golden barrier between
oneself and death felt to the carbon, through the tissue.
It rushes your sinuses and pulls your tendons. It will
warp the heart and bones and blood vessels. Death is a
flash flood that will crack your illusions like the
foundation of a house.

The deep, current-less pool of loss and grief washes us.
We are baptized into a life of small robberies.
Unanswered questions. Lost histories. Our parents
become sunken ships, unreachable in mystery.

The ability to feel how small you are on the surface of
the earth. See yourself from space, a camera panning
eternally back from your crown. Feel the planet turn
around you in it's full grace. Know that you are dust.

The doctor's flat voice and blank eyes. Her apology
clicking as sterile as the fluorescents. My mother wailing
through the tight air in the ill-named Family Room of the
emergency care unit. My mother collapsing into my
arms. Screaming and falling on a loop forever.

Her weight, the weight of a thirty year marriage, the mass of years, the cubic footage of a home, the size of separation; all settling onto my chest, all of it crashing down, a body falling into the sea.

The perpetual twilight of the ICU. Day and night bled into each other. Curled in the fetal position on the chair between the window and the bathroom, we slept in shifts. We cried into rough tissues and pissed into bleached toilets. We lived lifetimes in forty eight hours. Our friends and family drifted in and out. A tide of ghosts. Their quiet footsteps and outstretched limbs filled the air and built a halo around us. Soft whispers and wake-ups. The slide of clothing. The click of pens, echoing the clock, forever winding down. The orchestra of the machines breathing for my father. Collecting and measuring his urine and bile into plastic containers. Gathering the last bits of him. My father, emptying out of the world by the liter.

Millennia pass. Continents shift in uneasy beds. Unnamed species go quietly extinct. The unending heart of the world thumps madly on.

My sister fixes my father's hair with his beautiful crimson comb. His skin, always the color of summer, now pale and waxy. It does not look real. His body is so flat and so still. The only movement is the artificial rise and fall of his chest. There is stubble growing on his slender cheeks, and I wonder, nonsensically, if his face itches.

My sister is weeping and lovingly combing his sandy-brown hair, which was just beginning to show wisps of silver. She is gently pushing it into shape less than an inch away from his drowned mind.

All of him is lost to the rogue wave. The sudden, unthinkable cataclysm that pulled him to the bottom of the sea. A whirlpool. A Kraken. A red whale.

The doctor comes in. The doctors come in. They are waiting for us to let go, because that's all there is left for us. I sit, holding my dad's hand, and pressing the driving callouses at the base of each digit. My mother is asleep on a bench in the hall. My sister is asleep in a chair at the foot of his hospital bed.

I am whispering "I am so sorry."

I walk through the front door of my parents' house, and know that he will never walk through that door again. I open the closet. I bury my face in his coat. Fine leather and cigarettes. Wool and soft cologne. My father smelled like the quiet dusk of a library. I cry the bewildered, nervous tears of a child who has lost her parent in a crowded pavilion.

I pull the cigarettes my dad wasn't supposed to be smoking out of the inside breast pocket of his jacket. The red cardboard slides open like a shocked mouth. Full pack. Last pack. I take one out. I walk back out onto our porch, where we had stood beside each other in comfortable silence many times, and I light his cigarette.

We are a ring of salt. The doctors have come and gone. They have removed the tubes, and his body is running out. I am sitting at his left hand, holding it in mine as it slowly cools. This hand that cradled me, I cradle for the last time. The room is full of people who love us, and I can feel their hearts filling and emptying behind me. The green lines on the monitor over my sister's shoulder grow more shallow. Peaks and valleys become hills and ditches as everything slows down. The gears are quieting. No screeching halt, no crash; just the winding down of an elegant mechanism.

Everyone is crying. The world is emptier.

Concrete & Magnets

No matter what I am drawing, I am drawing you. The ink creeps up the page, and I am helpless to stop the curve of your jaw. The swing of your sidelong gaze spills out of my hands, The slight upturn of your arrogant nose and the soft gate of your lips, parted and smiling. You, in ink and watercolor and oils. You in chemicals. You, smudged on my hands and face, staining my clothes. The long winter when I knew you loved me fills the paper.

I am running from you and to you, always. I live in a circle. A closed circuit of want and regret, both currents feeding into my fingertips and lighting up the sleepless hours.

Longing drags it's feet up and down the dim halls of daydreams. I drive. I imagine you looking out of the passenger window. Tell me what you're seeing. Describe it as only you can. Make me know you all over again. I love you, still and always. When I get to Heaven, I will squint at the brightness and ask for you by name.

If This, Then That

I am bent in a chair at the end of her bed in the ICU. I can feel the no-color plastic of the chair sealing itself to my lower back. I am waiting on dawn for the morning shift and the surgical consult, while her bed inflates and deflates.

I am listening to the ice chips in the small styrofoam cup on her tray table softly collapse on themselves. The room is too cool for sleep. Minutes pass between blinks. I can feel my eyelids scraping across red sclera. I touch my fingertips together as a silhouette passes the curtained glass wall. I slide lower and watch my mother breathe.

There is nothing I can do. There is nothing to stop the words that will have to come from my mouth in the morning. And the next day. The words that will shift the world. Pull pavement out from under my sister's feet as she hunts the city. Bring my aunts racing from their corners of the planet. Bring our family's small circle of close friends to lock down around us like a phalanx, once again.

I am out of my depth. Flailing. I am only reacting. Reacting and replaying. Combing over the timeline to make sure I did everything I could.

Mom, your shirt is on inside-out.

Mom, your food is falling off the plate.

Mom, why is your house a mess?

Where did all of this come from?

You asked me that...four times. Yes.

The ER doctors and nurses were kind. They were efficient. They came to my mother. They came to me. They came to my sister.

Brain cancer is not what I was expecting to hear. Spanish Inquisition. The black corona with it's halo of tentacles. Reaching outwards towards the bent canyon of memory in the center of her head. The pictures are ugly. The name of the hungry, stupid monster is ugly.

Summer roared at it's reflection with the mouths of golden lions, in the way that only Summer in the northeast can, but it should have been snowing. The world should have hidden it's face in shame for it's cruelty. Blanketed and small like my mother's body under sterile white. The ground should have frozen. All growth should have halted; nature should have shut it's savage mouth, shocked at it's oversight.

Every tree should have shed it's leaves in mourning like a widow tearing her clothes.

And so, I was the crier. I counted breaths. I exhaled despair. On the world, I set a diaspora of heartbreak.

After the talking, there was only reacting. Only moving. Everything comes unhinged.

Planet Earth Is Blue

My mother lays upside-down on her bed like an inverted tarot card. She is covered in blood spots and machinery.

She is exhausted from screaming. The psychotic episodes surrounding the shower have been getting progressively worse. Her hygiene is suffering. Nobody tells you this. Doctors never mention that your mother, a woman who once prided herself on cleanliness and organization - a tower of righteous sanitary habits - would devolve into a shrieking toddler when told that she has to brush her teeth and wash her body.

Her shipwrecked body. She is The House of Swords and The Star.

Her speech is failing. She doesn't want to eat. She refuses water, both in and out. She no longer wipes herself properly. My mother scratches at her skin until it bruises. She picks her nose and ears and teeth with shaking, shameless hands.

A thousand, thousand indignities fall out of the sky like a rain of arrows, blotting out the sun.

To be forced stand by and watch someone disintegrate is to truly know love. It is holding your head up while being run through the heart.

For every shameful loss and slight that shows it's venomous teeth, you must be that much more noble. To feel the sand of your mother's existence slip through your hands as you sometimes scramble and sometimes freeze. To let it loom, and be unafraid. That is the love of a child for a dying parent.

All barriers fall away between the first death and the second. The first death came like a wave. Like an invading army. It smoothed the sand on the shores of my mother's memory, and then blew great craters in the landscape. The simpler, more understandable death; The death that is uniform and complete and unquestionable, will bookend this disgraceful limbo.

This half-light we are stumbling through.

I press my palms together and applaud the void. God covers his ears.

Repeater Volume III

The hospital bed breathes more steadily than my mother. She pulls the air of the ICU through tired tunnels. Her hands are swollen and static. Mucus pools in her mouth and throat. She cannot clear her own airway. The nurses come in and suction her mouth, and she winces. This is her only interaction with the world, now.

I want her to wake up and be her again. I see it in my mind. She flutters her eyes and recognizes me. Recognizes Rachel. Sees the atrocities committed against her and her family by her sisters and her "best friend".

I see my mother seeing everything.

The refined notes of the machines sound off sporadically when her oxygen saturation sinks below a certain number. When her blood pressure rises above a certain number. When her respiration varies too much in either direction. My mother is a fragile thing in a bracket of color-coded digits.

Nothing here echoes. In a place of great weight, sound falls to the floor like shattered iron. Our syllables are soldered to the grit on the tile. The stains on the walls rend heavy metals from our language. I sink into survival mode and grip tightly the memory of the sun above and the sand below. I am anywhere but here. I am not smelling this temple of goodbyes.

I pace the ward, and every open door reveals a vignette of despair.

The lawyers entrusted with her care by the court of New Jersey have done nothing but collect paychecks. They look on, either impotent or unwilling, as interlopers ravage what is left of my family.

The rage inside of me radiates outward and manifests itself in different ways. I have stopped taking care of myself. The prospect of brushing my teeth and showering every day is overwhelming, but I do at least that, still. I no longer care to cut my hair, and my glasses have been broken for months. I eat poorly, if I eat at all, and mostly I just rent my food. I am bloated and in pain most of the time, now.

My chest sometimes tightens, and I pray for a heart attack to take me down. There are long stretches of minutes, now, where I can feel my heart throb like a rotting tooth in my ribs. The first few times, I felt a sense of panic, but now, I just quietly debate whether knocking my fist against my chest is worth the effort.

My family is being murdered, and I can do nothing to stop it at this moment.

I have watched the mountain of my mother wear away to grit in the wind of cancer and the floods that our enemies brought to our door. They degrade us. They tell us our mother did not love us. Their cruelty goes unchecked by anyone in power. We take it, knowing that we have the truth. That we caught them stealing from a dying woman.

Their tantrums are the prelude to their real outrage. I cannot fathom the backlash that will pour out from them once they realize how trapped by their own self-dealing they truly are. They will claw for our eyes as the heavy net of the law, cast wide, falls down around them.

We don't flinch. We will not relent.

The body of death sits before us, still and patient. Life rolls out her hips and opens her arms. We will walk away with her.

Things have been stolen from us that cannot be replaced. Moments in my family's history that can never, ever come back. Every moment that passes is a slamming door, and there is no respite.

A Taken-Down Star

We were a family with the architecture of an August thunderstorm, we were sudden and fierce in our love and hatred for one another. We were many things. An island in a relentless northern sea. A burrow of badgers. A soft place to land. We were a theater and the players up on the stage and the audience and the curtain. We were every piece of each other's humanity, mirrored and amplified. It wasn't always good, but it wasn't all bad.

Solder And Fuse

I can feel the pieces, the broken things, shifting around inside as I move through the world. If I shake apart, I will not be surprised. Only curious to see what was making all of that godawful noise. I sometimes wonder if the sharp things, the things that feel like shards of glass and hot metal will just burst forth from my chest like so much reverse shrapnel.

One year and eight months as an orphan.

Falling Through Concrete

The public school system in rural-turned suburban New Jersey was a hastily-bolstered, flimsy dam shored up by the flash flood of cash by way of White Flight.

In kindergarten, the gauntlet opens. The social strata is still magmatic, ever shifting, never stable. Children like uranium isotopes. Unstable, trivalent, tetravalent, bonding and breaking. The fusion of best friends. The fission of first cliques.

Grade school would forge us into beautiful weapons.

I don't think our teachers in 1988 thought we would live to see adulthood.

The After You

You were born in the late afternoon on a day that was not yours.

I remember your feet. Tiny. Wriggling little landlocked fish. Creased and red. A band-aid made for an adult on one bruised heel no bigger than a thumb, eclipsing your joints up to the softness of your shin.

That is my first memory of you. Not the plastic box you slept in under the constant watch of the medical staff for two terrible weeks. Not your face. Not your smell. Your tiny feet sticking out of a blanket covered in pastel giraffes.

I remember our grandparents raising me up to see you, days before. Holding my body against the glass and pointing frantically. I didn't see you then, much to their disappointment and my confusion.

There. There that's her. Don't you see? This might have been my very first lie. I did not see you then. I didn't see you among the rows of the other infants. I remember nodding, but knowing they knew I didn't see you.

That is only part of what I have of you though. That is nothing compared to the awe of you.

What I truly have; what I will never lose, is being brought home to the house we would grow up in. The house of future wars and endless instability was so far away from that moment.

Mom on their bed. Dad downstairs, resting on the worn couch, and the very clear warmth of the golden autumn light through the crescent window. Mom holding you, the smallest and quietest thing. The most fragile piece of almost-being. You didn't cry. You never cried. You were as thoughtful as a favorite cat.

I remember your tiny feet, the size of mom's hands as she held you in her arms. Your fragile arms and your eyes that looked at all things at once, seeing the golden spiral in each flash of light. In each face.

Even at 4, we understand sacred. We know holy when we see it.

I asked to hold you, and I can still feel you in my arms. I can feel your body against my chest and asleep in my elbows. With each sibling born, a spade is placed in the headwaters of great rivers, and the eldest becomes more than just running water, coursing on a steady path.

We become deltas. places where wild things grow. Where sand and salt and unreachable secrets dwell.

Jealousy and fragmented rivalry followed. Our mother did not do well in sharing her attention.

People repeat their pain.

Orphan Planet (Epilogue and Preface)

I am thirty-four years old.
I cannot remember the last time someone held me.
I cannot remember the last time I felt romantic love.
I have days that are lost to ennui and loneliness.
I communicate mostly through text or messaging my
increasingly-distant population of friends online.
I am becoming two very different people.
A bifurcation of self is taking place.

New York Repeater Volume I

Leonard Cohen spoke to me last night about the perils
of residual Reaganomics in a culture vacuum.

I asked him about life existing outside of the event
horizon, constantly collapsing on itself. Microwaved
dinners and reality TV.

"Your food shouldn't beep at you, Allison."
He took a long drag off a Virginia Slim.

"You smoke women's cigarettes, Len. You don't get to
tell me how to eat my heat."

"Your dad smokes these, now."
A mute swan stretches its wings in the corner.

David Bowie woke me up with coffee and a danish this morning.
Stood thoughtfully beside my bed with a pink hospital tray.
He handed me a copy of the New York Native from 1981.
I'm not usually one for sweet breakfasts.

I eye the danish.

I like the acid of strong coffee to flush the sleep from between my teeth, and nothing else.

He asks questions about the growing popularity of arm band culture in a post-racial America. His laugh is soft and easy.

"Dave, you sang a song which explicitly states that you're afraid of Americans. We're afraid of Americans, too."

"If you're not going to eat that, I will, Allie. Your mum'll never know. You've been afraid your whole life. You were afraid in the womb."

He taps the May 18th headline and looks at me with two sets of eyes.

Outside, the sun is shining through a forest of tornadoes.

They are solid and still.

Debbie Harry and Freddie Mercury
Are sitting in the parlor
Of my small manhattan apartment

It is 1977
The year is a white cat
Asleep on a stack of The New York Times

Though Fred prefers The Post
Debbie is drinking gin
Freddie; a small glass of vermouth and bitters
Says his stomach hurts from the Television
the piano track from Good Old Fashioned Loverboy is
playing softly

We are on the third floor
earthbound enough for the traffic to
Slip through the walls
Under the door
Close enough to the sky to speak loud at heaven and be
heard

Debbie laughs
Pours more beefeater over slivers of ice

Freddie leans forward in an ancient wing chair to feel
the sun on his face
He smiles rabbit-toothed mischief

David Byrne left his glasses on my kitchen counter
Post-long afternoon nap
He took them off
for a good cry
at the end of the old war
And the beginning of the new war

He wiped his tears with a cashmere sleeve
and told me nothing stays
He should be back this evening
With groceries from Lombardi's
And wine from the nameless bodega on third.

My parents met
at Capulets

On Montague
in Brooklyn.

Not long from now.
Not far from here.

They left me all this recall on vinyl.
left me parallel lines and talking heads
Gave me a night at the opera.

The mad world spins
on its indifferent axis
I walk down avenues
Through echoes
Where they planted their busy feet and

It is sometimes so hard to believe that they ever existed

but
I turn corners in the villages both east and west
and I see them

portraits painted on lucite
And laid over a landscape
An animation cell
Frozen in the same gesture forever
A skipping record.

Golden Ratio

Give me the webbing
between your
Thumb and index finger
Where the evolution sits

Where the long memories
of lost ancestors
sing Kaddish

From throats
that once bloomed with gills
From cells that once only understood
The sunshine

Give me your least favorite mole
In your most exposed spot
And I'll give you my lip prints
My fingerprints

Give me the ghosts of your pregnancy

The striations
Archeological

That whisper the story of your multitude Across the holy
alluvial of your belly

Give me the hard pads
of your marathon feet
The paper lantern creases of the backs of your knees
The stretched self-inflicted perforations in your earlobes

Give me the shipmaker-white notches
Of your nailbeds
Give me the baptismal basin of your hips
The cathedral of your pelvic structure
All of you that performs a function
And holds a history
And echoes down the line

Calendula

To explain you
Is to paint the curl at
The corner of your mouth
When you are about to make yourself laugh

And the rose barbs of your warring teeth
When you are excited

At me
At anything

Over sound systems and full plates
I have been told you are beautiful
This is an objective truth
Empirical as blue sky and green summer.

objectivity is ankle deep

They don't know what your skin holds
What the unpaved crimson-earthed back roads of your
capillaries
And the golden radius of the villus hairs on your cheeks

can hold

I know your body
is not the mortar
but the pestle
Built to grind the world down to fiefdoms and darkness

In the charging twin engines of your symmetry

I am translated from tea leaves
like whispers through a wall

echoes down a hall

The neighborhood stands still and tilts an ear
Listens for us tonight in this dying summer belly heat

Your body is history
Your heart is graceful antique
Your words are heirlooms
I collect
And catalogue
And study through a lens

I hold my breath
I dig my heels into the shore
At the edge of a vast expanse
I wait
Anxious
To feel the root system of your hand in mine

I know your ballast
what keeps you on top of the water
I know your mercury

Apology IV

A seed left on a countertop
Spider down the drain

I push myself against the soundproof glass of our love
Every future that could have been

And howl your name to the hole in the sky

I carve memory
after memory
into my palms

With anxious fingernails
that once filled your back
with crescent moons

Everything that blooms in me
Turns towards the light of you

I am a field on fire, now
I am a burning river

And I will no longer
blacken your sky

Snapshot of Deepest, Most Inescapeable New Jersey, December 2015

There is an abalone shell filled with cigarette butts
Like broken fingers
On the sideboard

This particular day
is a table
piled high with hospital records
and henges of pill bottles
and coffee rings like rusted bulls-eyes
that blot out the heaviest words

But not enough
Nothing can fully eclipse this

This winding down of the war
The air is rabid

florescent bars
they flicker when we turn the coffee pot on
make our shadows sway

The flat smack of my bare feet on these new
construction floors
Nothing echoes here.
There is no history but the one of your suffering
Which has been logged and categorized and reported
from beginning to end, it was written

Somewhere we are happy

But not here

Love Poem That You Kept

If I could live only in the deep jungle scent of your hair
Where no light filters down to the forest floor

Where footsteps are soft
Where the rhythm is your own heart on grass and lichen
I would make camp and open my lungs to the tantrum
breeze of you

If there were a canopy to be had it would be your broad
arms
And the delicate punctuation of your fingers
The impatient Morse of your wrists and palms speaking

In tongues, in tongues handling serpents

There is balm in the valleys of you
Alluvial and rolling
The landscapes of you

Syllables like soft arrows

They fly from your Grecian lips and
Ancient heart that curls like the pacific

The animals
that live in the zenith
of your sleeping chest,
rising and falling

Apex predators

lazing on stones in the fierce sun of your smile

mute birds with plumage
used only for ritual wishing

Incandescent, wild-patterned things
who covet the light

Damned and settled
to the Mariana
in the sea of you
Illuminated like manuscripts in your deep trenches

NJ Transit Hymn

I was on my way

To beg forgiveness

When a train that was not scheduled
Approached my platform

I turned my attention to my thighs
And oiled through the hissing doors

Past spent commuters
Everything about them is tired
Their shoes
Deodorant
Briefcase handles

I'd been watching a bee struggle on the hand rest of a
bench.
It will die as I reach my terminus.

I'd already bought my ticket
At a machine that spoke to me
In the radiowave dream of a woman's voice

On this June day
In late spring
The rain launching itself at my crown
And shoulders

Everything around me moving at terminal velocity

I think about the path of water
And inevitability

And gravity
And descendants

Head east until the land ends
Head east until the world ends
Head east to the savage wilderness

The water will take us all back.

The woman in the handicapped seat says to the
conductor

I wish it would stop raining, you know?

He turns the volume down on his walkie,
cracking like the first notes of overhead thunder

And says

It's just beginning again

New York Repeater Volume II

It was in the forest of man where I met you.

There was snow on the ground.

NYC Exile seeks warm native roots for night blooming.
It's not my fault.
I was swept off to the wastelands when I was a baby.
I never belonged there.
Powerhouse seeks grounding.
I'm going to fall into Manhattan.
The only woman who opens her arms every time I
return.
I was frozen up to my knees, when I met you.
I was salted up to my thighs, folded under the table.

NYC expat seeks non-spiritualist for mutual reality
checks.
Repatriation imminent.
Will trade the secrets of savages for subway lessons.
Will share knowledge regarding how to tie knots in
lengths of rope

How to fix cars
How to paint walls

I can show you how to bury your parents.
In exchange for the nearest place to sit

the streets run east
and avenues run north.
I have it.

It was in the forest of man where I met you.
There was snow on the ground.

And even on the tiniest of the naked branches.
I was frozen up to my knees, when I met you.
I was salted up to my thighs, folded under the table.
In a hot restaurant. Everything was close.

You were close

Your hands were doing most of the talking
and then you were moving things to another table
a close table
your mouth was on mine
you were trying me on
making sure
that I would fit.
and I did.
For a while.

New York Old Blood Once Removed seeks casual
anonymity for long walks unnoticed.
Seeks the stability of in-born wealth with the conscience
of the AIDS generation.
You were always an inevitability and I was always
apologizing.
Will exchange sweat for the ability to remain aloof
Swap tears and other body fluids (upon request) for a
perfectly raised eyebrow
and a genius straight tie.

There was snow on the ground.
There was ice up to my palms.
You kissed me

and sealed me to the city forever.

A carousel, A Straight Line

I couldn't fall back to sleep so I ghosted tracks
Through wildest Brooklyn where
pleated-scarved commuters fear to tread
Carol King came with me.
Told me I'm the only one.

The silhouettes on the raised platform of the L
Blur like waterlogged barcodes
Like dune grass from home
The train runs on wild horses
Hooves, steelheavy, across and down
Winter smoke from unleathered muzzles

I wrap my wrist
like I am burying my fingers
In the coarse mane
of all of God's geldings
Carol sings to me from the abattoir

In the bomb shelter i have built around myself
I hum along to the flat air
the acoustics here are lonesome
and I still want to fuck a Soviet

Everything's underground
And in sealed jars
Everything is waiting to burst forth
Nothing makes me feel like you anymore

In the white light of bodega doorways
The sister borough
always feels like it just rained
Even when the grit is swirling
It sits on skin

If you turned Brooklyn on her head
And shook her by the ankles

To empty her pockets
What would fall into the river

The whores, the trees, this subway car,
the dollar roses and tomorrow's paper
All the headlines that can't keep up
Every missed call and meter maid
All the guns and us
Washed out to the womb of the Atlantic

Made in the USA
Middletown, DE
26 February 2021

34439079R10043